What Kids Wonder
about God and the Bible

Mary J. Davis

LEGACY PRESS®

To all of God's precious children everywhere. May this book answer your questions and give you the desire to search out your own answers in God's Word.

To Miss Clueless, Miss Ding, Miss Dong, Miss Kermit and Miss Jo. Also to Karen. Thanks to all of the kids at Camp Lookout, summer of 1998. Special thanks to Miss Clueless, Spiritual Life Teacher.

Thanks also to the children at Keokuk Christian Academy for your help. I love you all.

MY ANSWER JOURNAL
©2008 by Legacy Press, fifth printing
ISBN 10: 1-885358-72-5
ISBN 13: 978-1-885358-72-1
Legacy reorder #: LP46931
JUVENILE NONFICTION / Religion / Devotion & Prayer

Illustrator: Barbara Rodgers

Legacy Press
P.O. Box 261129
San Diego, CA 92196

Unless otherwise noted, Scriptures are from the
Holy Bible: New International Version (North American edition),
©1973, 1978, 1984 by the International Bible Society.
Used by permission of Zondervan Bible Publishers.

Printed in the United States of America

Table of Contents

Introduction

Do you ever have questions you want to ask God? Like why bad things happen to nice people? Or if angels are real? Or how you can deal with problems? Sometimes life seems confusing. Events around us are frightening. God seems far off.

God is always there for you to talk to. He loves and cares for you! This journal will help you answer questions that you have about God. You will be led to open your Bible for answers to all of life's questions.

The book begins with a collection of questions from real kids. You might even find your question right in that chapter! But if you don't, there are seven more sections of questions and answers that will probably include yours. If you still don't get the answers you need, talk to your parents, your pastor or a friend who is knowledgeable about God and the Bible.

<u>How to Use This Book</u>

The Question

Read the question and think about a time you might have asked this question.

Answers from the Word

Scriptures from the Bible will help you find the answer to the question. Read all of the verses. Underline or highlight those that are especially meaningful to you and help you understand God's will.

Think About the Word

This is a reflection on the Scriptures that will help you understand them and how to put God's Word into your everyday life. You will be asked to write some things on the blank lines.

In My Own Words

After reading the Scriptures and thinking about them, write the answer to the question in your own words.

Talk to God

Pray this prayer, and add to it what you feel you want to say to God.

More of God's Word

These are additional Scriptures to read that relate to the topic. Following the references are more questions for you to answer.

Words to Remember

This is a memory verse. When you put God's Word into your heart, you will always have something positive to think about even when things seem to go wrong. Write down the memory verse and place it where you can see it often. Try to memorize every Scripture in this journal.

People were bringing little children to Jesus to have him touch them, but the disciples rebuked them. When Jesus saw this, he was indignant. He said to them, "Let the children come to me, and do not hinder them, for the kingdom of God belongs to such as these. I tell you the truth, anyone who will not receive the kingdom of God like a little child will never enter it." And he took the children in his arms, put his hands on them and blessed them.
Mark 10:13-16

Your Questions

Dear God,
I love You. I know I am going to heaven someday to be with You. Will I be able to see, hear and touch You in heaven? If so, I want to give You a big hug.
Love, Ashley W.

Dear God,
Are You Spirit-like, or do You kind of look like us?
I love You, Alex L.

Answers from the Word

Then the man and his wife heard the sound of the Lord God as he was walking in the garden in the cool of the day, and they hid from the Lord God among the trees of the garden.

— Genesis 3:8

The Lord God made garments of skin for Adam and his wife and clothed them. And the Lord God said, "The man has now become like one of us, knowing good and evil.

— Genesis 3:21-22

The Son is the radiance of God's glory and the exact representation of his being, sustaining all things by his powerful word. After he had provided purification for sins, he sat down at the right hand of the Majesty in heaven.

— Hebrews 1:3

Think About the Word

In Genesis 3:8, God made a sound as He walked through the garden. This tells us that God has some feeling for cool and warm, and some physical traits. In Genesis 3:21, what did God do for Adam and Eve? gave them garments
Of skin and told right and wrong

In Genesis 22, how had man become? Men
become one of us evil
knowing good and evil

Read 1 Samuel 6:19-20. People were struck down because they simply looked into the ark of the Lord! Now go to Hebrews 1:3 and 1 Corinthians 15:35-55. What does Jesus look like in heaven? *like his human form*

What will we look like in heaven? *we will look like spiritual*

In My Own Words

I think we will look like an angel

Talk to God

God, I understand now how we will all look in heaven. I think that I will be able to touch You, hug You and be close to You as much as I want. I will praise Your name forever, just as all the heavenly angels are doing now. I love You, God. Amen.

More of God's Word

Genesis 1:1-2
Genesis 1:27

What I learned: *That this book is conusing*

The verse that best answered the question: *15:3*

More questions: *got none*

Words to Remember

And he took the children in his arms, put his hands on them and blessed them.

— Mark 10:16

Dear God,
Why do people turn away from You so easily? I know someone who got mad at the preacher and won't come to church anymore. My friend's dad won't go to church anymore because he didn't like something he heard in a sermon.

Love, Colin

Dear God,
My friend's parents won't take her to church anymore because someone at church made them mad. Why do people stay away from You because of one little thing?

With love, Your friend Jenna

Answers from the Word

This righteousness from God comes through faith in Jesus Christ to all who believe. There is no difference, for all have sinned and fall short of the glory of God.

— Romans 3:22-23

Let us not give up meeting together, as some are in the habit of doing, but let us encourage one another — and all the more as you see the Day approaching.

— Hebrews 10:25

Watch out for false prophets.

— Matthew 7:15

For false Christs and false prophets will appear and perform great signs and miracles to deceive even the elect.

— Matthew 24:24

Think About the Word

Read John 6:60-70. Some of Jesus' followers turned back because of some of his teachings. Write out verse 69.

we believe and know that you are the Holy one of God

Read Romans 3:22-23. How should we feel when one person has sinned against us? Are we without sin ourselves?

_____

Write out Hebrews 10:25.

_____

_____

Write a pretend letter to someone who has stopped going to
church. Tell the person that God wants him or her in church,
and that a small problem should not keep the person away.

In My Own Words

_____

_____

Talk to God

Father, I will remain faithful to You all my life. Amen.

More of God's Word

Luke 8:4-15
Luke 14:15-23

What I learned: _____

The verse that best answered the question: _____

More questions: _____

_____

Words to Remember

*Anyone who breaks one of the least of these commandments and
teaches others to do the same will be called least in the kingdom of
heaven, but whoever practices and teaches these commands will be
called great in the kingdom of heaven.*

— Matthew 5:19

Dear God,
You know everything, even the future. If You know what we are going to do even before we do it, why do You expect us to make choices? Why don't You just cause us to do the right thing?
I love You, Michelle O.

Dear God,
How do You know what I am going to do, even though I didn't do it yet?
Love, Richard

Answers from the Word

This then is how we know that we belong to the truth, and how we set our hearts at rest in his presence whenever our hearts condemn us. For God is greater than our hearts, and he knows everything. If our hearts do not condemn us, we have confidence before God and receive from him anything we ask, because we obey his commands and do what pleases him. And this is his command: to believe in the name of his Son, Jesus Christ, and to love one another as he commanded us. Those who obey his commands live in him, and he in them. And this is how we know that he lives in us: We know it by the Spirit he gave us.
— 1 John 3:19-24

Think About the Word

Read all of Genesis chapter 3. Adam and Eve chose to eat the fruit that God forbade them to eat. Doing that, their eyes were opened to good and evil. Before then, everything in the garden of Eden was paradise.

Read 1 John 3:19-24. Verse 20 says that God is greater than _____. Our hearts condemn us. Our desire for sinning gets us into trouble.

Write out verse 23.

_____

_____

Now think of the Genesis verses and the 1 John verses together. People chose to commit the first sin. After that, if God had taken over our ability to choose, we would not be able to choose to believe in Christ. God does know all that we do, but He gives us free will to choose. That way, we are able to choose to be God's children and follow His ways. We are able to choose to repent and be redeemed by God.

In My Own Words

_____

_____

_____

Talk to God

God, I am glad to be Your child. I choose to follow Your ways and stay on the right path. Amen.

More of God's Word

Romans, chapter 8. This chapter talks about the Spirit, who is in us. We have the Spirit to help us make right choices. The Spirit will nudge our conscience when we are about to do something wrong.

What I learned: _____

_____

The verse that best answered the question: _____

More questions: _____

_____

Words to Remember

The Spirit himself testifies with our spirit that we are God's children.

— Romans 8:16

Dear God,
Why does my family always argue?
Love, Karl

Dear God,
Why does my big sister hate me? What can I do to make her stop treating me mean?
Love, Karen

Answers from the Word

Be imitators of God, therefore, as dearly loved children and live a life of love, just as Christ loved us and gave himself up for us as a fragrant offering and sacrifice to God.

— Ephesians 5:1-2

Think About the Word

Read all of the Scriptures on these two pages, including Words to Remember at right. What does God expect of us? _____

_____

What is the greatest commandment? (Matthew 22:37) _____

_____

If someone treats you badly, what is the best way to treat him or her?_____

_____

Who can help you with a situation that is hard for you?

_____

Don't forget to pray!

In My Own Words

_____

_____

_____

Talk to God

God, I will try harder to have good relationships. I will try not to start arguments. Help me to be the kind of person who glorifies You all of the time. Amen.

More of God's Word

1 John 3:18
Colossians, chapter 3

What I learned: _____

_____

The verse that best answered the question: _____

More questions: _____

_____

Words to Remember

Dear friends, let us love one another, for love comes from God.
Everyone who loves has been born of God and knows God.
— 1 John 4:7

Dear God,
I have always wondered this: How would the world be if Adam and Eve hadn't eaten from the forbidden tree?

Love, Allyson

Answers from the Word

Genesis 2:4-20
Genesis 3:16-19

Think about the Word

Look up and read the Scriptures above. What was it like in the garden of Eden?

_____

_____

What are some things that God put upon man and woman because of the sin they committed?

_____

_____

Read Genesis 2:15 again and compare it to Genesis 3:17-19.

In My Own Words

_____

_____

_____

Talk to God

God I want to follow Your ways and serve You. I love You. Amen.

More of God's Word

Read the account of creation and the fall of man in Genesis chapters 1-3.

What I learned: _____

_____

The verse that best answered the question: _____

More questions: _____

_____

Words to Remember

God saw all that he had made, and it was very good.

— Genesis 1:31

Dear God,
I would like to know just how You got here. Who or what created You?
Love, Erin

Dear God,
Where did You come from? This is a hard question for me to figure out.
Love, Avery M.

Answers from the Word

In the beginning was the Word, and the Word was with God, and the Word was God.

— John 1:1

You created all things, and by your will they were created and have their being.

— Revelation 4:11

Think About the Word

We can find in the Bible from where and when everything came! Everything! What does it say about God? He was there at the very beginning. The Creator was not created by anyone or anything. The Creator is our great and wonderful God! There was a beginning to all earthly things, as there will be an end, but there is no beginning or end to God.

In My Own Words

_____

_____

_____

Talk to God

God, You are the beginning and end of all things. You are eternal, and that makes me feel wonderful. I know that You are in control of everything, and that all is well as long as You are there for me. Amen.

More of God's Word

Revelation 1:8
Psalm 102:25-26

What I learned: _____

_____

The verse that best answered the question: _____

More questions: _____

_____

Words to Remember

In the beginning God created the heavens and the earth.

— Genesis 1:1

◉

Dear God,
People keep telling me that the world will end on a certain day. I hear all the time that You are coming back very soon. Is that true?
Love, Misty M.

Dear God,
Will the world really end in fires, floods, volcano eruptions and explosions? Will I be here when that happens?
Love, Shawn

Answers from the Word
Matthew 24:36
Luke 21:25-28
2 Peter 3:10-18

Think About the Word

Look up and read all of the Scriptures above. Does anyone know when the end will be? _____

Who does know? _____

Write out 2 Peter 3:9. _____

_____

In My Own Words

_____

_____

_____

Talk to God

God, I know You wish for everyone to repent and become Your child. You don't want anyone to miss being in heaven with You. I love You and I will tell others about You. Amen.

More of God's Word

Read all of 2 Peter.

What I learned: _____

_____

The verse that best answered the question: _____

More questions: _____

_____

Words to Remember

With the Lord a day is like a thousand years, and a thousand years are like a day. The Lord is not slow in keeping his promise, as some understand slowness. He is patient with you, not wanting anyone to perish, but everyone to come to repentance.

— 2 Peter 3:8-9

Dear God,
Were there once things on the earth like unicorns and dinosaurs?
Love, Brandi

Dear God,
Were there really giants?
Love, Lucas

Answers from the Word
Genesis 6:4
Numbers 23:22 and 24:8
Joshua 12:4 and 15:8
Psalm 29:6
Isaiah 27:1
Ezekiel 29:3
Job 39:9 and 10

Think About the Word
Look up each Scripture above in the King James version of the Bible. What did you find out about each of these:

unicorns _____

dinosaurs/dragons _____

giants _____

In My Own Words
_____
_____
_____
_____

Talk to God

God, You created great and wonderful things. It is fun to think about all of the different things on earth, even if they are no longer here. I love You, Lord. Amen.

More of God's Word

Deuteronomy 33:17
Psalm 22:21
Isaiah 34:7
Deuteronomy 2:20
Numbers 13:33

What I learned: _____

_____

The verse that best answered the question: _____

More questions: _____

_____

Words to Remember

The earth is the Lord's, and everything in it, the world, and all who live in it.

— Psalm 24:1

Dear God,
Will we ever see a cure for cancer?
Love, Heidi

Dear God,
Will AIDS ever be cured?
Love, Monica

Dear God,
Are You ever going to heal all the bad diseases?
Love, Courtney

Answers from the Word

Jesus went throughout Galilee, teaching in their synagogues, preaching the good news of the kingdom, and healing every disease and sickness among the people.
— Matthew 4:23

He said, "If you listen carefully to the voice of the Lord your God and do what is right in his eyes, if you pay attention to his commands and keep all his decrees, I will not bring on you any of the diseases I brought on the Egyptians, for I am the Lord, who heals you."
— Exodus 15:26

…To another gifts of healing by that one Spirit.
— 1 Corinthians 12:9

But the crowds learned about it and followed him. He welcomed them and spoke to them about the kingdom of God, and healed those who needed healing.
— Luke 9:11

By the power of signs and miracles, through the power of the Spirit. So from Jerusalem all the way around to Illyricum, I have fully proclaimed the gospel of Christ.
— Romans 15:19

Think About the Word

All of the Scriptures above deal with healing. Jesus healed many people, and so did His disciples. God allowed the healings so that people would know that He is God. Many diseases through the years have been healed. Polio was once a crippling and frightening disease. Now, a vaccine protects children from polio. Many cancers can be detected and healed. Scientists are making new discoveries constantly that may lead to a cure for AIDS. Yes, God may choose to heal all disease in our lifetime. It is certain that He cares enough for us that He allows scientists to cure some of these horrible diseases.

In My Own Words

_____

_____

Talk to God

Lord, I know someone with cancer [fill in with a situation you know]. This person has fought a hard battle, but now is cancer-free. I thank You for Your miracles. I thank You for doctors and scientists who are putting an end to some of these terrible diseases. Amen.

More of God's Word

Ecclesiastes 3:1
Psalm 103:1-6

What I learned: _____

_____

The verse that best answered the question: _____

More questions: _____

_____

Words to Remember

I will bless them and the places surrounding my hill. I will send down showers in season; there will be showers of blessing.
— Ezekiel 34:26

God, Jesus and the Holy Spirit

Where did God come from?

Answers from the Word

In the beginning God created the heavens and the earth.

— Genesis 1:1

"Holy, holy, holy is the Lord God Almighty, who was, and is, and is to come." The living creatures give glory, honor and thanks to him who sits on the throne and who lives for ever and ever.

— Revelation 4:8-9

"You are worthy, our Lord and God, to receive glory and honor and power, for you created all things, and by your will they were created and have their being."

— Revelation 4:11

Think About the Word

The whole earth praises God for being the Creator. God was there to begin with, before everything thing else. He was not created by anyone or anything. If He had been created by something or someone else, how could He be praised and honored as the Creator? Write a song to give God the glory and honor and thanks for being our Creator.

_____

_____

In My Own Words

_____

_____

_____

Talk to God

God, You are awesome! It is comforting to know that You

always were and always will be there. Nothing is going to happen to me or the world that is not totally in Your plan. I love You! Amen.

More of God's Word

Read these Scriptures about God:

Revelation 21:6-7
Revelation 22:13
1 John 2:13-14, 24
Jeremiah 10:11-13

What I learned: _____

_____

The verse that best answered the question: _____

More questions: _____

_____

Words to Remember

"Holy, holy, holy, is the Lord God Almighty, who was, and is, and is to come."

— Revelation 4:8

How long will God live?

Answers from the Word

The Lord is the true God; he is the living God, the eternal King.
— Jeremiah 10:10

He is the true God and eternal life.
— 1 John 5:20

Your statutes stand firm; holiness adorns your house for endless days, O Lord.
— Psalm 93:5

Stand up and praise the Lord your God, who is from everlasting to everlasting.
— Nehemiah 9:5

Think About the Word

How long do you think eternal and everlasting are?

_____

Draw a circle on a separate sheet of paper. Where does the circle begin? Where does it end?

_____

_____

Everlasting is like the circle…no beginning and no end. Look up Revelation 22:13 and write it here. Write below it: God will NEVER end.

_____

_____

In My Own Words

_____

_____

_____

Talk to God

Oh, Father, I am so glad to have confidence in You. You are everlasting! You are eternal! And, best of all, You are MY God! Amen.

More of God's Word

Read these Scriptures about how long God will live:
Genesis 21:33
Psalm 41:13
1 Kings 9:3
Revelation 1:8 and 21:6

What I learned: _____

_____

The verse that best answered the question: _____

More questions: _____

_____

Words to Remember

Trust in the Lord forever, for the Lord, the Lord, is the Rock eternal.
— Isaiah 26:4

Were You Alone before creating the world?

Answers from the Word

The Spirit of God was hovering over the waters.

— Genesis 1:2

In the beginning was the Word, and the Word was with God, and the Word was God. He was with God in the beginning.

— John 1:1-2

Think About the Word

Which three were here when the world was created?

_____

_____

Genesis 1:2 says God's Spirit was there. John 1:1-2 says that Jesus (the Word) was there. Write the three names below that represent the Trinity.

_____

In My Own Words

_____

_____

_____

Talk to God

God, I know You are actually three in one. You have Your Spirit, which You have given to all of us. And Jesus was with You in the beginning. I love You and am thankful for You and all You have done for me. Amen.

More of God's Word

All of Genesis, chapter 1
John 1:1-5
Numbers 11:16-17
Luke 1:35

What I learned: _____

_____

The verse that best answered the question: _____

More questions: _____

_____

Words to Remember

Then God said, "Let us make man in our image."

— Genesis 1:26

Who is the Holy Spirit?

Answers from the Word

And the Spirit of God was hovering over the waters.
— Genesis 1:2

We are witnesses of these things, and so is the Holy Spirit, whom God has given to those who obey him.
— Acts 5:32

Now the Lord is the Spirit.
— 2 Corinthians 3:17

I [John] baptize you with water, but he will baptize you with the Holy Spirit.
— Mark 1:8

As Jesus was coming up out of the water, he saw heaven being torn open and the Spirit descending on him like a dove.
— Mark 1:10

When you send your Spirit, they are created.
— Psalm 104:30

Peter replied, "Repent and be baptized, every one of you, in the name of Jesus Christ for the forgiveness of your sins. And you will receive the gift of the Holy Spirit. The promise is for you and your children and for all who are far off—for all whom the Lord our God will call."
— Acts 2:38-39

Think about the Word

Whose Spirit is the Holy Spirit? _____

Where was the Holy Spirit when God created the world?
_____

Where is the Holy Spirit now? (See Psalm 139:7, Mark 1:10 and Acts 5:32.) _____

Do we have the Holy Spirit today? (See Acts 2:38-39.)
_____
_____

In My Own Words

_____

_____

_____

Talk to God

Lord, I am thankful that Your Spirit works in my life. He was present at creation and is present in my life now. Thank You for Your Spirit. Amen.

More of God's Word

Exodus 31:3
Exodus 35:31
Isaiah 59:21
Ezekiel 2:2
Matthew 1:18
Matthew 3:11

What I learned: _____

_____

The verse that best answered the question: _____

More questions: _____

_____

Words to Remember

Where can I go from your Spirit? Where can I flee from your presence? If I go up to the heavens, you are there; if I make my bed in the depths, you are there.

— Psalm 139:7-8

Is Jesus the same as God?

Answers from the Word

Through him all things were made; without him nothing was made that has been made.

— John 1:3

What about the one whom the Father set apart as his very own and sent into the world? Why then do you accuse me of blasphemy because I said, "I am God's Son"? Do not believe me unless I do what my Father does. But if I do it, even though you do not believe me, believe the miracles, that you may know and understand that the Father is in me, and I in the Father.

— John 10:36-38

The angel answered, "The Holy Spirit will come upon you, and the power of the Most High will overshadow you. So the holy one to be born will be called the Son of God.

— Luke 1:35

Think About the Word

Read John 1:3 above. Who would you say that Jesus is?

_____

_____

Now read the Scriptures below John 1:3. Who would you say that Jesus is? _____

_____

In fact, Jesus is both of these things. He is God, and He is God's Son. Jesus was with God from the beginning. Look up and read John 1:1-3 and Luke 1:35.

In My Own Words

_____

_____

Talk to God

God, I thank You for Jesus. Thank You for all You have done for me. Amen.

More of God's Word

Psalm 2:7-12
Hebrews 1:3-13

What I learned: _____

_____

The verse that best answered the question: _____

_____

More questions: _____

_____

Words to Remember

For to us a child is born, to us a son is given, and the government will be on his shoulders. And he will be called Wonderful Counselor, Mighty God, Everlasting Father, Prince of Peace.

— Isaiah 9:6

What is God like?

Answers from the Word

Look up each Scripture below and write one or two words that describe God:

1 John 4:16 _____

Genesis 17:1 _____

Joshua 22:22_____

Deuteronomy 4:31 _____

Exodus 20:5 _____

Psalm 24:10 _____

Nehemiah 9:17 _____

Jeremiah 25:33_____

Psalm 8:1 and 9 _____

Isaiah 40:28 _____

Psalm 46:1 _____

Numbers 16:46 _____

Jeremiah 32:18_____

2 Samuel 22:4_____

Psalm 2:5 _____

Daniel 9:9_____

Think About the Word

Which words about God surprised you?

_____

Write a tribute to God, using as many of the words listed above as you can.

_____

_____

In My Own Words

_____

_____

_____

Talk to God

God, You are my God. I praise Your wonderful name. Amen.

More of God's Word

Genesis 28:3   *Psalm 103:4*

Joshua 24:19   *Ezekiel 5:15*

Luke 6:36   *2 Corinthians 1:2*

What I learned: _____

_____

The verse that best answered the question: _____

More questions: _____

_____

Words to Remember

Ascribe to the Lord, O mighty ones, ascribe to the Lord glory and strength. Ascribe to the Lord the glory due his name; worship the Lord in the splendor of his holiness.

— Psalm 29:1-2

Is God Always with Me?

Answers from the Word

The Lord is my strength and my shield; my heart trusts in him, and I am helped.
— Psalm 28:7

We wait in hope for the Lord; he is our help and our shield.
— Psalm 33:20

David said about him: "I saw the Lord always before me. Because he is at my right hand, I will not be shaken."
— Acts 2:25

God has said, "Never will I leave you; never will I forsake you."
— Hebrews 13:5

Think About the Word

Read Psalm 28:7 and 33:20. Who is our help?

_____

_____

What else is He in those verses?

_____

_____

Read Acts 2:25. What does it say about God helping us?

_____

_____

Write out Hebrews 13:5.

_____

_____

Write about a time when you knew God was helping you.

_____

_____

My Own Words

_____

_____

_____

Talk to God

God, You are ALWAYS with me. I know it. I have confidence that You are always there. Thank You. Amen.

More of God's Word

Isaiah 58:11
Psalm 18:2
Joshua 1:5
Deuteronomy 31:8

What I learned: _____

_____

The verse that best answered the question: _____

More questions: _____

_____

Words to Remember

Surely I am with you always, to the very end of the age.
— Matthew 28:20

Does God Do Miracles Today?

Answers from the Word

Now to each one the manifestation of the Spirit is given for the common good. To one there is given through the Spirit the message of wisdom, to another the message of knowledge by means of the same Spirit, to another faith by the same Spirit, to another gifts of healing by that one Spirit, to another miraculous powers, to another prophecy, to another distinguishing between spirits, to another speaking in different kinds of tongues, and to still another the interpretation of tongues. All these are the work of one and the same Spirit, and he gives them to each one, just as he determines.
— 1 Corinthians 12:7-11

God also testified to it [salvation] by signs, wonders and various miracles, and gifts of the Holy Spirit distributed according to his will.
— Hebrews 2:4

Think About the Word

Who gives the gifts described in the Scriptures?

_____

_____

Who chooses the ones who will receive these gifts? _____

Many people believe that the time of miracles and other wondrous works is past. But look around you. Do you see some miracles that only God could have had a hand in? Do you know someone who was healed? What other kinds of wondrous things do you see around you? How would you describe a miracle? If someone asked you if God performs miracles today, how would you answer?

_____

_____

_____

_____

@

My Own Words

_____

_____

_____

Talk to God

Lord, I know people believe different ways about some of Your works. But I just want to thank You for the things around me that I am sure are Your miracles. It is not important whether I believe the way everyone else in the world believes. It is important that I put my trust in You and allow You to work in my life. Amen.

More of God's Word

Acts 14:3
Deuteronomy 10:21
Psalm 9:1
Joel 2:30

What I learned: _____

_____

The verse that best answered the question: _____

More questions: _____

_____

Words to Remember

There are different kinds of gifts, but the same Spirit. There are different kinds of service, but the same Lord. There are different kinds of working, but the same God works all of them in all men.
— 1 Corinthians 12:4-6

Are angels real?

Answers from the Word

Are not all angels ministering spirits sent to serve those who will inherit salvation?

— Hebrews 1:14

He [Jacob] had a dream in which he saw a stairway resting on the earth, with its top reaching to heaven, and the angels of God were ascending and descending on it.

— Genesis 28:12

Men ate the bread of angels; he sent them all the food they could eat.

— Psalm 78:25

In the sixth month, God sent the angel Gabriel to Nazareth, a town in Galilee.

— Luke 1:26

But after he had considered this, an angel of the Lord appeared to him in a dream.

— Matthew 1:20

Think About the Word

According to the Scriptures above, what are angels?

_____

Where do angels live?

_____

Do angels eat?

_____

Do they have names?

_____

What are some ways that God uses angels?

_____

What do you imagine that they look like?

_____

In My Own Words

_____

_____

_____

Talk to God

Dear God, I like to read about angels in Your Word. You have used these heavenly beings for Your glory. I love that You also use me for Your glory. Amen.

More of God's Word

Hebrews, chapter 1
Mark 1:13
1 Timothy 3:16
2 Thessalonians 1:7

What I learned: _____

_____

The verse that best answered the question: _____

More questions: _____

_____

Words to Remember

You have come to Mount Zion, to the heavenly Jerusalem, the city of the living God. You have come to thousands upon thousands of angels in joyful assembly.

— Hebrews 12:22

Does God still love me when I misbehave?

Answers from the Word

Sow for yourselves righteousness, reap the fruit of unfailing love.
— Hosea 10:12

The Lord disciplines those he loves.
— Hebrews 12:6

Whoever has my commands and obeys them, he is the one who loves me.
— John 14:21

For all have sinned and fall short of the glory of God, and are justified freely by his grace through the redemption that came by Christ Jesus.
— Romans 3:23-24

Think About the Word

What should we sow? _____

_____

Think of righteousness as "rightness." Then what will we get in return?

_____

What does Hebrews 12:6 say that God does?

_____

How do we show that we love God?

_____

Write a letter to God, thanking Him that you are saved and justified through Jesus.

_____

_____

_____

_____

In My Own Words

_____

_____

_____

Talk to God

Lord, sometimes I just blow it. I sin. I let someone convince me to sin, or I do something wrong on my own. Please forgive me. Help me to think about Jesus' sacrifice for me. I am truly sorry for my actions, Lord. Amen.

More of God's Word

Proverbs 3:12; 12:1; 13:24
John 16:27
Luke 15:7,10
1 John 4:12

What I learned: _____

_____

The verse that best answered the question: _____

More questions: _____

_____

Words to Remember

For God so loved the world that he gave his one and only Son, that whoever believes in him shall not perish but have eternal life. For God did not send his Son into the world to condemn the world, but to save the world through him. Whoever believes in him is not condemned.
— John 3:16-18

How do I please God?

Answers from the Word

Look up the Scriptures below and write one or two words that answer the question above.

Proverbs 15:8 _____

Deuteronomy 4:2 _____

Psalm 26:8 _____

Psalm 31:23 _____

Psalm 52:9 _____

Joshua 24:15 _____

Matthew 28:19-20 _____

1 John 3:22 _____

Colossians 3:13 _____

Think About the Word

Write a paragraph that tells how you can please God.

_____

_____

_____

_____

In My Own Words

_____

_____

_____

Talk to God

Lord, I want to do no less than to please You everyday. I love You and will do my best to please You in all I do. Amen.

More of God's Word

Ecclesiastes 2:26
Isaiah 56:4
John 8:29
Ephesians 5:10
1 Timothy 2:3

What I learned: _____

_____

The verse that best answered the question: _____

More questions: _____

_____

Words to Remember

We are not trying to please men but God, who tests our hearts.
— 1 Thessalonians 2:4

God's Word

Why was God's Word written?

Answers from the Word

Faith comes from hearing the message, and the message is heard through the word of God.

— Romans 10:17

From infancy you have known the holy Scriptures, which are able to make you wise for salvation through faith in Christ Jesus.

— 2 Timothy 3:15

When I am afraid, I will trust in you. In God, whose word I praise, in God I trust; I will not be afraid.

— Psalm 56:3-4

Think About the Word

According to the Scriptures, what are some reasons that God's Word was written?

_____

_____

Write about a time when God's Word helped you.

_____

_____

In My Own Words

_____

_____

_____

Talk to God

I love Your Word, Lord. I love to read, study and learn from the Bible. It makes me feel closer to You and helps me obey You. Amen.

More of God's Word

Exodus 20:1-24

What I learned: _____

_____

The verse that best answered the question: _____

More questions: _____

_____

Words to Remember

All Scripture is God-breathed and is useful for teaching, rebuking, correcting and training in righteousness, so that the man of God may be thoroughly equipped for every good work.

— 2 Timothy 3:16

can kids understand the Bible?

Answers from the Word

Look up and read each of the passages below. Then write a sentence that describes what you read.

Numbers, chapters 22 and 23: _____

_____

1 Kings, chapter 18: _____

_____

Joshua, chapter 10: _____

_____

Think About the Word

The Bible is filled with things God wants us to know — you understood the stories above, didn't you? Children are commanded to live godly lives. Many people think the Bible is stuffy and hard to read, but you can see from the stories you just read that the Bible is interesting for all ages. You can learn a lot about God by reading His Word.

In My Own Words

_____

_____

_____

Talk to God

Lord, I thank You for Your Word. I enjoy reading the stories that are in Your Word. I love to learn more about You. Amen.

More of God's Word

Judges 15:4-5
Judges 16
Acts 20:7-12

What I learned: _____

_____

The verse that best answered the question: _____

More questions: _____

_____

Words to Remember

But if anyone obeys his word, God's love is truly made complete in him.
— 1 John 2:5

How was God's word written?

Answers from the word

All Scripture is God-breathed.

— 2 Timothy 3:16

We did not follow cleverly invented stories when we told you about the power and coming of our Lord Jesus Christ...Above all, you must understand that no prophecy of Scripture came about by the prophet's own interpretation. For prophecy never had its origin in the will of men, but men spoke from God as they were carried along by the Holy Spirit.

— 2 Peter 1:16, 20-21

The word of the Lord came to me.

— Jeremiah 1:4

The word of the Lord that came to Hosea.

— Hosea 1:1

The word of the Lord came to the prophet.

— Zechariah 1:1

The Lord has spoken this word.

— Isaiah 24:3

Think About the word

Who gave the apostles the words to tell people?

_____

How did God get His Word to the people?

_____

Write about a time when you heard a sermon and you were sure the preacher was talking directly to you.

_____

_____

_____

In My Own Words

_____

_____

_____

Talk to God

Thank You for Your Word, Father. Thank You for giving Your Word to people, so that we can all study and learn to follow You. Amen.

More of God's Word

Psalm 4 and 110 (read the sub headings to see who wrote it)
Song of Songs 1:1
Jeremiah 1:1-4
Ezekiel 1:1
Amos 1:1
Luke 1:1-4

What I learned: _____

_____

The verse that best answered the question: _____

More questions: _____

_____

Words to Remember

Man does not live on bread alone but on every word that comes from the mouth of the Lord.

— Deuteronomy 8:3

Is God's Word all true?

Answers from the Word

As for God, his way is perfect; the word of the Lord is flawless.
— 2 Samuel 22:31

And the words of the Lord are flawless, like silver refined in a furnace of clay, purified seven times.
— Psalm 12:6

As for God, his way is perfect; the word of the Lord is flawless.
— Psalm 18:30

Think About the Word

Like the finest of silver that is purified many times, God's words are flawless. Flawless means without error or without imperfection. God is perfect, and His words are flawless. What is something you can compare God's perfection to? Silver, gold, diamonds? Write what is perfect about something that you like, then write how God's Word is even more perfect.

_____

_____

In My Own Words

_____

_____

_____

Talk to God

Father, Your Word is not only always true, it is without error. You are perfect and Your Word is flawless. I praise You and Your Word. Amen.

More of God's Word

Deuteronomy 32:4
Ephesians 1:13
Ephesians 6:17

What I learned: _____

_____

The verse that best answered the question: _____

More questions: _____

_____

Words to Remember

Every word of God is flawless; he is a shield to those who take refuge in him. Do not add to his words, or he will rebuke you and prove you a liar.
— Proverbs 30:5-6

Can anyone change God's Word?

Answers from the Word

Your word, O Lord, is eternal; it stands firm in the heavens.
— Psalm 119:89

Your laws endure to this day, for all things serve you.
— Psalm 119:91

I warn everyone who hears the words of the prophecy of this book: If anyone adds anything to them, God will add to him the plagues described in this book. And if anyone takes words away from this book of prophecy, God will take away from his share in the tree of life and in the holy city, which are described in this book.
— Revelation 22:18-19

Do not add to his words.
— Proverbs 30:6

Think About the Word

How long will God's Word last?_____

What will happen to anyone who adds to God's Word?
_____

What will happen to anyone who takes away from God's Word?
_____

What is the warning in Proverbs 30:6?_____
_____
_____

Write some ways that someone might try to change God's Word. What do you think God would do? _____
_____
_____

In My Own Words

_____

_____

_____

Talk to God

Dear God, I love You and Your Word. Thank You that no one can change Your word without great punishment. I feel secure knowing that You will not allow someone to change Your eternal Word. Amen.

More of God's Word

Psalm 119:160
Romans 16:25-27

What I learned: _____

_____

The verse that best answered the question: _____

More questions: _____

_____

Words to Remember

Because God wanted to make the unchanging nature of his purpose very clear to the heirs of what was promised, he confirmed it with an oath.
— Hebrews 6:17

Why Should I read God's Word?

Answers from the Word

"I tell you the truth, whoever hears my word and believes him who sent me has eternal life and will not be condemned; he has crossed over from death to life.

— John 5:24

How can a young man keep his way pure? By living according to your word. I seek you with all my heart; do not let me stray from your commands.

— Psalm 119:9-10

I have hidden your word in my heart that I might not sin against you.

— Psalm 119:11

Bind them upon your heart forever; fasten them around your neck. When you walk, they will guide you; when you sleep, they will watch over you; when you awake, they will speak to you. For these commands are a lamp, this teaching is a light, and the corrections of the discipline are the way to life.

— Proverbs 6:21-23

Think About the Word

What if we didn't have the Bible? How would we know what God expects of us? How would we even know there is a God? How would we know there is a heaven? Write why you feel you need to read God's Word.

_____

_____

_____

In My Own Words

_____

_____

_____

Talk to God

God, I know I should read Your Word. I will try harder to read a little from my Bible each day. Thank You for Your Word to teach and guide me. Amen.

More of God's Word

Psalm 119: 11, 16, 25
Deuteronomy 6:8
Deuteronomy 11:18
2 Kings 10:6
Psalm 119:97-104

What I learned: _____

_____

The verse that best answered the question: _____

More questions: _____

_____

Words to Remember

Blessed rather are those who hear the word of God and obey it.
— Luke 11:28

Your word is a lamp to my feet and a light for my path.
— Psalm 119:105

⊚

God's World

Why did God create the world and people?

Answers from the Word

Everyone who is called by my name, whom I created for my glory, whom I formed and made.

— Isaiah 43:7

Created to be like God in true righteousness and holiness.
— Ephesians 4:24

The earth is the Lord's, and everything in it, the world, and all who live in it.

— Psalm 24:1

Think About the Word

Who created everyone? Why?

_____

_____

Ephesians 4:24 says we are created to be like _____.

To whom does the earth belong? To whom do we belong?

_____

In My Own Words

_____

_____

_____

Talk to God

You are my God, I am Your child. Thank You for creating me. Amen.

More of God's Word

Psalm 102:18-22

What I learned: _____

_____

The verse that best answered the question: _____

More questions: _____

_____

Words to Remember

I will give them a heart to know me, that I am the Lord. They will be my people, and I will be their God, for they will return to me with all their heart.

— Jeremiah 24:7

Why is the world full of trouble?

Answers from the Word

We know that we are children of God, and that the whole world is under the control of the evil one. We know also that the Son of God has come and has given us understanding.

— 1 John 5:19-20

Jesus said to his disciples: "Things that cause people to sin are bound to come."

— Luke 17:1

Through these he has given us his very great and precious promises, so that through them you may participate in the divine nature and escape the corruption in the world caused by evil desires.

— 2 Peter 1:4

Think About the Word

How did sin enter the world? _____

_____

Who controls the world? _____

_____

What is bound to come? _____

_____

What causes corruption in the world? _____

_____

In My Own Words

_____

_____

_____

Talk to God

Lord, although the world seems full of trouble, I know You are there to protect from sin and from hurt by evilness. I love You. Amen.

More of God's Word

Romans 1:29-30

What I learned: _____

_____

The verse that best answered the question: _____

More questions: _____

_____

Words to Remember

Therefore, just as sin entered the world through one man, and death through sin, and in this way death came to all men, because all sinned.
— Romans 5:12

Why are there starving people, wars and killing?

Answers from the Word

Jesus answered: "Watch out that no one deceives you. For many will come in my name, claiming, 'I am the Christ,' and will deceive many. You will hear of wars and rumors of wars, but see to it that you are not alarmed. Such things must happen, but the end is still to come. Nation will rise against nation, and kingdom against kingdom. There will be famines and earthquakes in various places. All these are the beginning of birth pains.

— Matthew 24:4-8

If the Lord is with us, why has all this happened to us?...The Lord answered, "I will be with you."

— Judges 6:13, 16

I have set the Lord always before me. Because he is at my right hand, I will not be shaken.

— Psalm 16:8

Think About the Word

Sometimes it seems that trouble is all around. Floods and famine, earthquakes and wars — these things seem to devastate many nations. In an age when we have televisions and computers, we see these troubles on a daily basis.

Write out Judges 6:17._____

_____

Write out Psalm 16:8. _____

_____

Write a letter to convince someone that God is in control and He will never ever leave us. _____

_____

@

In My Own Words

_____

_____

_____

Talk to God

God, I am confident that You are there. Everything that happens in the world is for Your purpose. I trust You. Amen.

More of God's Word

Luke 21:5-28

What I learned: _____

_____

The verse that best answered the question: _____

More questions: _____

_____

Words to Remember

See to it that you are not alarmed.

— Matthew 24:6

Dear Friend,
God is King of this earth. He will never leave us. We can always pray to Him because He loves us.

Love,
Me

Where do I find joy in the troubled world?

Answers from the Word

The Lord knows how to rescue godly men from trials.
— 2 Peter 2:9

For the Lord your God will bless you in all your harvest and in all the work of your hands, and your joy will be complete.
— Deuteronomy 16:15

Come, let us sing for joy to the Lord; let us shout aloud to the Rock of our salvation. Let us come before him with thanksgiving and extol him with music and song. For the Lord is the great God, the great King above all gods.
— Psalm 95:1-3

Think About the Word

Who do you think provides our joy? _____

_____

Who rescues us or goes with us through trials? _____

_____

What does God expect us to do in order to have joy?

_____

How do we come before God? _____

_____

Read Psalm 92. List some praise words. _____

_____

List some things for which you can praise God. _____

_____

_____

In My Own Words

_____

_____

_____

Talk to God

Lord, I can have joy any time I want. You are always with me.
You rescue me; You guide me. I can create joy on a sad day just
by praising Your name! I love You. Amen.

More of God's Word

Isaiah 58:13-14
Psalm 113

What I learned: _____

_____

The verse that best answered the question: _____

More questions: _____

_____

Words to Remember

Every good and perfect gift is from above, coming down from the Father.
— James 1:17

Why did God create creepy things like spiders?

Answers from the Word

God made the wild animals according to their kinds, the livestock according to their kinds, and all the creatures that move along the ground according to their kinds. And God saw that it was good.
— Genesis 1:25

And the creatures of the field are mine.
— Psalm 50:11

Think About the Word

To whom does every creature belong? _____

Who chose to create every creature? _____

What did God say about all that He made?
_____

Write about something you think is creepy. What don't you like about it? What purpose do you think God had for making it?
_____
_____

In My Own Words

_____
_____
_____

Talk to God

Lord, I know You have a reason for everything You created. Some creatures are to feed others. Some are for beauty, while others are not so pretty in my eyes. Thank You for Your beautiful world. Amen.

More of God's Word

How many are your works, O Lord! In wisdom you made them all; the earth is full of your creatures.

Psalm 104:24

Let everything that has breath praise the Lord.

Psalm 150:6

What I learned: _____

_____

The verse that best answered the question: _____

More questions: _____

_____

Words to Remember

For everything God created is good, and nothing is to be rejected.
— 1 Timothy 4:4

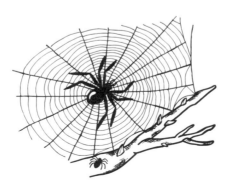

When and how will the world end?

Answers from the Word

No one knows about that day or hour, not even the angels in heaven, nor the Son, but only the Father.

— Matthew 24:36

When you hear of wars and revolutions, do not be frightened. These things must happen first, but the end will not come right away.

— Luke 21:9

Think About the Word

Read "Words to Remember" at right. What a wonderful way for the world to end! All of God's people will be gathered by angels. Many people today try to frighten God's people and make us think that the end of the world will be awful. Guess what? We won't be here to see it, because we will be gathered by the angels and taken to God's heaven. People also try to predict when the world will end. God's Word (Matthew 24:36) tells us that only God knows. People on earth do not know when the world will end. As always, God has a wonderful plan.

In My Own Words

_____

_____

_____

Talk to God

Lord, I will not let others worry me about when and how the world will end. I will concentrate on serving You, and let You take care of the world. I know it will be a wonderful day when Your angels gather all of Your people. Amen.

More of God's Word

Luke 21:25-28

What I learned: _____

_____

The verse that best answered the question: _____

More questions: _____

_____

Words to Remember

They will see the Son of Man coming on the clouds of the sky, with power and great glory. And he will send his angels with a loud trumpet call, and they will gather his elect from the four winds, from one end of the heavens to the other.

— Matthew 24:30

God's People

Is God sorry He made people?

Answers from the Word

The Lord was grieved that he had made man on the earth, and his heart was filled with pain.

— Genesis 6:6

Then Noah built an altar to the Lord and, taking some of all the clean animals and clean birds, he sacrificed burnt offerings on it. The Lord smelled the pleasing aroma and said in his heart: "Never again will I curse the ground because of man, even though every inclination of his heart is evil from childhood. And never again will I destroy all living creatures, as I have done. As long as the earth endures, seedtime and harvest, cold and heat, summer and winter, day and night will never cease."

— Genesis 8:20-22

And God sent an angel to destroy Jerusalem. But as the angel was doing so, the Lord saw it and was grieved because of the calamity and said to the angel who was destroying the people, "Enough!"

— 1 Chronicles 21:15

Think About the Word

In Genesis, God was sorry that He had made man on earth. Then came the flood. God cleansed His earth, saving only a few of each living creature, including people. Then God swore He would never destroy all living creatures. He had shown His wrath and His power.

Read 1 Chronicles 21:15. God sent an angel to destroy His sinful nation. But it was too much for God to bear. He still loved His people. He stopped the angel from killing all of His people.

These Scriptures show us that God hates all sin. But God loves His people!

In My Own Words

_____

_____

_____

Talk to God

Father, I know You hate sin, but You love Your people. I don't want to grieve You and make You sorry that You created me and chose me for Your very own. Please forgive me of my wrongs, and help me to be a careful follower of Your word. Amen.

More of God's Word

Psalm 33:18, 22
Ezekiel 14:12-23

What I learned: _____

_____

The verse that best answered the question: _____

More questions: _____

_____

Words to Remember

Let your face shine on your servant; save me in your unfailing love.
— Psalm 31:16

Why do some people not believe in God?

Answers from the Word

Even though I was once a blasphemer and a persecutor and a violent man, I was shown mercy because I acted in ignorance and unbelief.
— 1 Timothy 1:13

The god of this age has blinded the minds of unbelievers, so that they cannot see the light of the gospel of the glory of Christ, who is the image of God.
— 2 Corinthians 4:4

Do not harden your hearts as you did at Meribah, as you did that day at Massah in the desert, where your fathers tested and tried me, though they had seen what I did.
— Psalm 95:8-9

Think About the Word

Why would someone turn away from God?

_____

_____

Read 1 Timothy 1:13. This is Paul speaking. Before he began to follow Christ, why did he curse God and all believers?

_____

_____

In 2 Corinthians, who has blinded the minds of unbelievers? Who do you think the god of this age might be?

_____

_____

In Psalm 95:8-9, who hardened the hearts of God's people?

_____

We find in these verses two reasons that people do not believe in and follow God: 1. Satan hardens hearts against God and 2. People harden their own hearts against God.

Write a prayer to tell God you will never harden your heart against Him. _____

_____

_____

In My Own Words

_____

_____

_____

Talk to God

God, I love You. I would never purposely turn against You. Please help me to remain Your strong follower all my life. Amen.

More of God's Word

2 Corinthians 6:14
2 Timothy 2:19

What I learned: _____

_____

The verse that best answered the question: _____

More questions: _____

_____

Words to Remember

See to it, brothers, that none of you has a sinful, unbelieving heart that turns away from the living God.

— Hebrews 3:12

Why did people live so long in the Old Testament?

Answers from the Word

Altogether Methuselah lived 969 years.

— Genesis 5:27

When men began to increase in number on the earth and daughters were born to them, the sons of God saw that the daughters of men were beautiful, and they married any of them they chose. Then the Lord said, "My Spirit will not contend with man forever, for he is mortal; his days will be a hundred and twenty years."

— Genesis 6:1-3

Think About the Word

Read "Words to Remember" at right. What did God tell the people of earth to do?_____

How old was Methuselah when he died? He was the oldest man to ever live! _____

Why did God shorten the life span of people?

_____

In My Own Words

_____

_____

_____

Talk to God

Lord, I love to read about the beginning of the world. I love to learn how You created people and gave them Your earth to live on. Thank You, God. Amen.

More of God's Word

Genesis 5:1,2
Isaiah 45:12

What I learned: _____

_____

The verse that best answered the question: _____

More questions: _____

_____

Words to Remember

God blessed them and said to them, "Be fruitful and increase in number; fill the earth."

— Genesis 1:28

Why are there different colors of skin?

Answers from the Word

Can the Ethiopian change his skin?
— Jeremiah 13:23

On his way he met an Ethiopian eunuch, an important official in charge of all the treasury of Candace, queen of the Ethiopians. This man had gone to Jerusalem to worship.
— Acts 8:27

Think About the Word

An Ethiopian is a person who comes from a certain region. God made people distinguishable for their region. Just as today, people from certain parts of the world look different than people from other parts. Write a praise poem to God that is dedicated to people of all skin colors.

_____

_____

In My Own Words

_____

_____

_____

Talk to God

Lord, I know You created each of us in Your image, no matter what color my skin is. Thank You for creating each of us very special. Amen.

More of God's Word

Genesis 1:27

What I learned: _____

_____

The verse that best answered the question: _____

More questions: _____

_____

Words to Remember

The whole earth is full of his glory.

— Isaiah 6:3

Why did God make me look this way?

Answers from the Word

My frame was not hidden from you when I was made in the secret place. When I was woven together in the depths of the earth, your eyes saw my unformed body. All the days ordained for me were written in your book before one of them came to be.

— Psalm 139:15-16

The Lord does not look at the things man looks at. Man looks at the outward appearance, but the Lord looks at the heart.

— 1 Samuel 16:7

Think About the Word

Who formed us from the very beginning? _____

What was written in God's book? _____

_____

List 10 things you love about your appearance.

_____   _____

_____   _____

_____   _____

_____   _____

_____   _____

List 10 things you think God loves about you.

_____   _____

_____   _____

_____   _____

_____   _____

_____   _____

In My Own Words

_____

_____

_____

Talk to God

Lord, I know I am beautiful in Your sight. Sometimes I don't feel so beautiful, but I know You love me very much. Help me to always realize there is something beautiful about me. Amen.

More of God's Word

Psalm 33:13-15
Proverbs 31:30

What I learned: _____

_____

The verse that best answered the question: _____

More questions: _____

_____

Words to Remember

I praise you because I am fearfully and wonderfully made; your works are wonderful, I know that full well.

— Psalm 139:14

Why do I sin against God?

Answers from the Word

Let us throw off everything that hinders and the sin that so easily entangles.

— Hebrews 12:1

When tempted, no one should say, "God is tempting me." For God cannot be tempted by evil, nor does he tempt anyone; but each one is tempted when, by his own evil desire, he is dragged away and enticed. Then, after desire has conceived, it gives birth to sin.

— James 1:13-15

Think About the Word

What entangles us? _____

_____

Who cannot be tempted by evil? _____

_____

What are we tempted by? _____

_____

What does evil desire give birth to? _____

_____

My Own Words

_____

_____

_____

Talk to God

God, I know that sin comes from evil. I will try to stay away from all evil ways. I will try not to sin against You. Amen.

More of God's Word

1 John 5:17-20

What I learned: _____

_____

The verse that best answered the question: _____

More questions: _____

_____

Words to Remember

All have sinned and fall short of the glory of God, and are justified freely by his grace through the redemption that came by Christ Jesus.
— Romans 3:23-24

How does God feel about children?

Answers from the Word

Matthew 18:2, 4, 5, 16

Matthew 19:13-14

Luke 9:47-48

Mark 10:13-16, 24

Think About the Word

Practice your Bible skills by looking up each of the Scriptures above. Write a paragraph to tell how Jesus feels about children.

_____

_____

_____

_____

_____

In My Own Words

_____

_____

_____

Talk to God

I know You love me, Lord. I know I am very special to You. Thank You for loving children. Amen.

More of God's Word

1 John 2:28-3:10

What I learned: _____

_____

The verse that best answered the question: _____

_____

More questions: _____

_____

Words to Remember

I tell you the truth, anyone who will not receive the kingdom of God like a little child will never enter it.

— Luke 18:17

There are so many people, does God really know and care about me?

Answers from the Word

Cast all your anxiety on him because he cares for you.

— 1 Peter 5:7

Are not two sparrows sold for a penny? Yet not one of them will fall to the ground apart from the will of your Father. Even the very hairs of your head are all numbered. So don't be afraid; you are worth more than many sparrows.

— Matthew 10:29-31

Think About the Word

Underline "the will of your Father" in Matthew 10:29-31 above. This doesn't say that no sparrow falls without God knowing it, it says that no sparrow falls without it being God's will. God even knows how many hairs are on your head — He has carefully and lovingly numbered each one! Write a love letter from God to you. _____

_____

_____

_____

In My Own Words

_____

_____

_____

Talk to God

Father God, loving Lord, I know You care about me. In those times when I feel unloved or unimportant, help me to remember how much You really love me. I love You, too. Amen.

More of God's Word

Luke 12:6-10
Luke 12:27-28
Matthew 6:25-34

What I learned: _____

_____

The verse that best answered the question: _____

More questions: _____

_____

Words to Remember

The Lord is good, a refuge in times of trouble. He cares for those who trust in him.

— Nahum 1:7

Prayer

Does God hear every prayer?

Answers from the Word

For the eyes of the Lord are on the righteous and his ears are attentive to their prayer.   — 1 Peter 3:12

Cast your cares on the Lord and he will sustain you; he will never let the righteous fall.
                                                  — Psalm 55:22

Think About the Word

Who takes care of us? _____

Does God say we can only count on Him at certain times of the day? Is there a limit to how many times we can call on God? Of course not!

Write out at least one of the Scriptures above on a separate piece of paper. Place it where you can see it often.

Make a business card by cutting a piece of paper into a 3" x 2" rectangle. Write out Psalm 55:22 on one side. On the other side, write "1-800-GOD-HEARS." Keep your business card with you to remind you that God is always there to hear you.

In My Own Words

_____

_____

_____

Talk to God

I know You are always there to listen and watch over me, God. I feel great knowing You are there. Thank You. Amen.

🌀

More of God's Word

Psalm 55:17
Psalm 69:33
Psalm 145:17-20

What I learned: _____

_____

The verse that best answered the question: _____

More questions: _____

_____

Words to Remember

This is the confidence we have in approaching God: that if we ask anything according to his will, he hears us. And if we know that he hears us — whatever we ask — we know that we have what we asked of him.

— 1 John 5:14-15

What if I don't get the answer I want from God? How do I know He has answered?

Answers from the Word

If we ask anything according to his will, he hears us.

— 1 John 5:14

And if we know that he hears us – whatever we ask – we know that we have what we asked of him.

— 1 John 5:15

Think About the Word

In 1 John 5:14, how are we told we should ask God?

_____

_____

Does this tell you why God might say "No" in answer to some of your prayers? Why do you think He would say "no"?

_____

_____

Read Psalm 20 in your Bible. Write some words that help you know that God hears and answers your prayers.

_____

_____

In My Own Words

_____

_____

Talk to God

Lord, I know sometimes I ask You for something that might not be the right thing for me. I know only You can see what will happen to me in the future. I trust that You will provide what is best for me. I love You! Amen.

More of God's Word

1 Kings 8:45
1 Kings 8:49

What I learned: _____

_____

The verse that best answered the question: _____

More questions: _____

_____

Words to Remember

I call on you, O God, for you will answer me; give ear to me and hear my prayer.

— Psalm 17:6

Do I have to pray for everyone?

Answers from the Word

Brothers, pray for us.

— 1 Thessalonians 5:25

Therefore confess your sins to each other and pray for each other so that you may be healed. The prayer of a righteous man is powerful and effective.

— James 5:16

"But I tell you who hear me: Love your enemies, do good to those who hate you, bless those who curse you, pray for those who mistreat you.

— Luke 6:27-28

Think About the Word

Paul is asking for prayer in 1 Thessalonians 5:25. James is telling the churches to pray for each other in James 5:16.

In Luke 6:27 and 28, for whom are we to pray?

_____

_____

In My Own Words

_____

_____

_____

Talk to God

Lord, I understand that I should pray for all those around me. I am to pray even for my enemies. I will do that Lord, I promise. Amen.

More of God's Word

Hebrews 13:18
Colossians 1:3-14

What I learned: _____

_____

The verse that best answered the question: _____

More questions: _____

_____

Words to Remember

But I tell you: Love your enemies and pray for those who persecute you.
— Matthew 5:44

How Should I Pray?

Answers from the Word

When you pray, do not be like the hypocrites, for they love to pray standing in the synagogues and on the street corners to be seen by men. I tell you the truth, they have received their reward in full. But when you pray, go into your room, close the door and pray to your Father, who is unseen. Then your Father, who sees what is done in secret, will reward you. And when you pray, do not keep on babbling like pagans, for they think they will be heard because of their many words. Do not be like them, for your Father knows what you need before you ask him.

— Matthew 6:5-8

Pray continually.

— 1 Thessalonians 5:17

Give thanks in all circumstances, for this is God's will for you in Christ Jesus.

— 1 Thessalonians 5:18

Think About the Word

Read Matthew 6:5-8. What a silly picture that would make! Be sure not to pray like that.

Write out Matthew 6:8 and 1 Thessalonians 5:17.

_____

_____

In 1 Thessalonians 5:18, are we told to give thanks only when good things happen? _____

In My Own Words

_____

_____

_____

Talk to God

Father in heaven, I praise Your name and give You thanks. I love You and will always try to follow Your ways. Amen.

More of God's Word

Ephesians 6:18
Philippians 1:4
Jude 1:20

What I learned: _____

_____

The verse that best answered the question: _____

More questions: _____

_____

Words to Remember

Our Father in heaven, hallowed be your name, your kingdom come, your will be done on earth as it is in heaven. Give us today our daily bread. Forgive us our debts, as we also have forgiven our debtors. And lead us not into temptation, but deliver us from the evil one.
— Matthew 6:9-13

God's Church

What is the church?

Answers from the Word

And I tell you that you are Peter, and on this rock I will build my church, and the gates of Hades will not overcome it.
— Matthew 16:18

Greet also the church that meets at their house.
— Romans 16:5

And he is the head of the body, the church.
— Colossians 1:18

Now I rejoice in what was suffered for you, and I fill up in my flesh what is still lacking in regard to Christ's afflictions, for the sake of his body, which is the church.
— Colossians 1:24

Think About the Word

Is the church a building? _____

Who is the church? _____

Whose body are we? _____

Who is the head of the church? _____

In Romans 16:5, where did the church meet? Do we have to meet inside a fancy building to be the church?

_____

_____

My Own Words

_____

_____

_____

Talk to God

Jesus, You are the head of the church. I am part of that church, and I love You. Amen.

More of God's Word

Ephesians 5:25-32

What I learned: _____

_____

The verse that best answered the question: _____

More questions: _____

_____

Words to Remember

Just as each of us has one body with many members, and these members do not all have the same function, so in Christ we who are many form one body, and each member belongs to all the others.
— Romans 12:4-5

Why are there so many different churches?

Answers from the Word

1 Corinthians 1:10-17
1 Corinthians 12:12-27
Ephesians 4:1-7

Think About the Word

Look up and read the Scriptures above.

What kinds of divisions were the churches having in 1 Corinthians 1:10-17? _____

In 1 Corinthians 12:12-14, is the church made up of only one part? Write what Paul has to say about the church. _____

_____

Read Ephesians 4:4-6. _____

In My Own Words

_____

_____

_____

Talk to God

Father, help me to love all of my brothers and sisters in the Lord. Help me not to think someone is wrong for not being part of my kind of church. Amen.

More of God's Word

Read all of 1 Corinthians, chapters 12 and 13.

What I learned: _____

_____

The verse that best answered the question: _____

More questions: _____

_____

Words to Remember

Show proper respect to everyone: Love the brotherhood of believers, fear God, honor the king.

— 1 Peter 2:17

What rules does God have for the church and its leaders?

Answers from the Word

1 Timothy chapters 2 and 3

Think About the Word

What are some rules for worship you learned in these Scriptures? _____

_____

In My Own Words

_____

_____

_____

Talk to God

I love going to church, Father. I love and respect the leaders of my church. I love You. Amen.

More of God's Word

Romans 12:1
Hebrews 13:17

What I learned: _____

_____

The verse that best answered the question: _____

More questions: _____
_____

Words to Remember

Here is a trustworthy saying: If anyone sets his heart on being an overseer, he desires a noble task.

— 1 Timothy 3:1

Do I have to go to church?

Answers from the Word

Let us not give up meeting together, as some are in the habit of doing, but let us encourage one another — and all the more as you see the Day approaching.
— Hebrews 10:25

Worship the Lord with gladness; come before him with joyful songs.
— Psalm 100:2

Think About the Word

In Hebrews 10:25, what were some of the saints in the habit of doing? _____

What are we to do more of as we see the Day of Judgment approaching? _____

Write out Psalm 100:2. _____

_____

In My Own Words

_____

_____

_____

Talk to God

God, I sometimes grumble and complain about having to go to church. I really do love worshipping and learning in Your house, Father. Help me to encourage others to worship You also. Amen.

More of God's Word

Psalm 23:6
Psalm 26:8
Romans 12:1-3

What I learned: _____

_____

The verse that best answered the question: _____

More questions: _____

_____

Words to Remember

I rejoiced with those who said to me, "Let us go to the house of the Lord."
— Psalm 122:1

Being saved

Why is there death?

Answers from the Word
Romans 5:12-21
Genesis 6:3

Think About the Word

Read all of the Romans passage above. How did death enter into the world? _____

Who is credited for bringing death?_____

Who will bring life? _____

Why do we have hope even though death exists?

_____

Genesis 6:3 says that man is mortal. What do you think mortal means? _____

Does it seem that God planned for people to live forever on earth? _____

In My Own Words

_____

_____

_____

Talk to God

Father, death seems scary sometimes. But, I know I belong to You. Death is just traveling from this world to the wonderful eternity You have waiting for Your children. Amen.

More of God's Word

Read Isaiah chapter 59 about sin, confession and redemption.

What I learned: _____

_____

The verse that best answered the question: _____

More questions: _____

_____

Words to Remember

Now if we died with Christ, we believe that we will also live with him.
— Romans 6:8

Where will I go when I die?

answers from the Word

No one has ever gone into heaven except the one who came from heaven — the Son of Man. Just as Moses lifted up the snake in the desert, so the Son of Man must be lifted up, that everyone who believes in him may have eternal life. For God so loved the world that he gave his one and only Son, that whoever believes in him shall not perish but have eternal life. For God did not send his Son into the world to condemn the world, but to save the world through him.
— John 3:13-17

In my Father's house are many rooms; if it were not so, I would have told you. I am going there to prepare a place for you. And if I go and prepare a place for you, I will come back and take you to be with me that you also may be where I am. You know the way to the place where I am going.
— John 14:2-4

Praise be to the God and Father of our Lord Jesus Christ! In his great mercy he has given us new birth into a living hope through the resurrection of Jesus Christ from the dead, and into an inheritance that can never perish, spoil or fade — kept in heaven for you.
— 1 Peter 1:3-4

Think About the Word

Where did the Son come from? _____

_____

Why did God send His Son into the world? _____

_____

What is in God's house? _____

_____

For whom is Jesus preparing a place? _____

_____

In My Own Words

_____

_____

_____

Talk to God

God, I am so glad I have hope in You. I am so thankful that Jesus is preparing a place in heaven for me. Amen.

More of God's Word

1 Peter 1:3-12

What I learned: _____

_____

The verse that best answered the question: _____

More questions: _____

_____

Words to Remember

Do not let your hearts be troubled. Trust in God; trust also in me.
— John 14:1

What is salvation?

Answers from the Word

The kingdom of heaven is near.
— Matthew 10:7

And this is what he promised us — even eternal life.
— 1 John 2:25

Salvation belongs to our God, who sits on the throne, and to the Lamb.
— Revelation 7:10

For God did not appoint us to suffer wrath but to receive salvation through our Lord Jesus Christ. He died for us so that, whether we are awake or asleep, we may live together with him.
— 1 Thessalonians 5:9-10

Think About the Word

What is the wages of sin (Romans 6:23, at right)?_____
_____

Who gives us life? _____

What is near (Matthew 10:7)? _____

In 1 John 2:25, what are we promised?_____

In Revelation 7:10, to whom does salvation belong? _____

What is salvation (1 Thessalonians 5:9-10)? _____
_____

In My Own Words

_____
_____
_____

Talk to God

Lord, I am thankful for the salvation You have provided through Jesus. Amen.

More of God's Word

Romans 5:9
1 Corinthians 15:2

What I learned: _____

_____

The verse that best answered the question: _____

More questions: _____

_____

Words to Remember

For the wages of sin is death, but the gift of God is eternal life in Christ Jesus our Lord.

— Romans 6:23

How do I get saved?

Answers from the Word

Whoever believes and is baptized will be saved.

— Mark 16:16

And everyone who calls on the name of the Lord will be saved.

— Acts 2:21

Repent, then, and turn to God, so that your sins may be wiped out.

— Acts 3:19

Think About the Word

Read Mark 10:17-31. What did the young man ask Jesus?

_____

What did the young man say about keeping the
commandments in verse 20? _____

_____

What was the one other thing Jesus told the young man to do?

_____

Do you think verse 25 means that no one with money will go
to heaven? Jesus might be saying here that we should love
Him more than anything. If we are not willing to give up our old
ways and the material things we have for Him, then we cannot
devote ourselves to Him. What do you think this verse means?

_____

Read John 3:1-21. What does Nicodemus not understand in
verse 4? _____

_____

How does Jesus explain it to him? _____

_____

Read Acts 16:25-34. How did God use this situation to cause a whole family to become Christians? _____

_____

What is each one of us called to do? _____

_____

In My Own Words

_____

_____

Talk to God

God, I am so very glad to be one of Your children. I love You. I believe in You. I promise to follow You. Thank You for choosing me to be one of Your own. Amen.

More of God's Word

Acts 20:21
2 Peter 3:9
Titus 3:5
Ephesians 2:5, 8
John 10:9

What I learned: _____

_____

The verse that best answered the question: _____

More questions: _____

_____

Words to Remember

Repent and be baptized, every one of you, in the name of Jesus Christ for the forgiveness of your sins. And you will receive the gift of the Holy Spirit. The promise is for you and your children and for all who are far off — for all whom the Lord our God will call.

— Acts 2:38-39

How can I be sure I am saved?

answers from the Word

By this gospel you are saved, if you hold firmly to the word I preached to you.

— 1 Corinthians 15:2

Hebrews 6:13-20
Hebrews 10:35-39
2 Timothy 2:11-13

Think About the Word

Read all of Hebrews 6:13-20. What is it impossible for God to do?

_____

What does verse 19 say hope is? _____

Read Hebrews 10:35-39. What will be richly rewarded?

_____

What will we receive if we persevere? (Persevere means to not give up.)_____

When would God not be pleased with us? _____

_____

Read 2 Timothy 2:11-13. Complete the sentences:

If we died with him, we will _____.

If we endure, we will _____.

If we disown him, he will _____.

If we are faithless, he will _____.

In My Own Words

_____

_____

_____

Talk to God

Lord, I have learned in Your Word that I can be sure of being saved. I will follow You all my life and serve You the best that I can. I love You. Amen.

More of God's Word

Colossians, chapters 2 and 3

What I learned: _____

_____

The verse that best answered the question: _____

More questions: _____

_____

Words to Remember

He who stands firm to the end will be saved.

— Mark 13:13

What will happen at Jesus' second coming?

Answers from the Word

He (Christ) must remain in heaven until the time comes for God to restore everything, as he promised long ago through his holy prophets.
— Acts 3:21

At that time the sign of the Son of Man will appear in the sky, and all the nations of the earth will mourn. They will see the Son of Man coming on the clouds of the sky, with power and great glory. And he will send his angels with a loud trumpet call, and they will gather his elect from the four winds, from one end of the heavens to the other.
— Matthew 24:30-31

Look, he is coming with the clouds, and every eye will see him, even those who pierced him; and all the peoples of the earth will mourn because of him. So shall it be! Amen.
— Revelation 1:7

Think About the Word

Write out in your own words the promise that God has made to all His people about going to heaven. _____
_____

Why do you think the Scriptures from Matthew and Revelation say that the peoples of the earth will mourn? _____
_____

Do you think that means God's own people, or those who did not repent and become children of God?_____
_____

Who will come at the same time as Jesus?_____

What will they do? _____

In My Own Words

_____

_____

_____

Talk to God

I am glad to know how Jesus will return, Father. I am thankful that He will come to get me and all of His children. Amen.

More of God's Word

Matthew 26:64
Mark 13:26
Mark 14:62
1 Thessalonians 4:14-18

What I learned: _____

_____

The verse that best answered the question: _____

More questions: _____

_____

Words to Remember

For the Lord himself will come down from heaven, with a loud command, with the voice of the archangel and with the trumpet call of God, and the dead in Christ will rise first. After that, we who are still alive and are left will be caught up together with them in the clouds to meet the Lord in the air. And so we will be with the Lord forever.

— 1 Thessalonians 4:16-17

What is heaven like?

Answers from the Word

Stephen, full of the Holy Spirit, looked up to heaven and saw the glory of God, and Jesus standing at the right hand of God.
— Acts 7:55

Now we know that if the earthly tent we live in is destroyed, we have a building from God, an eternal house in heaven, not built by human hands.
— 2 Corinthians 5:1

Think About the Word

Read Revelation chapter 4 and chapter 22. Do you think heaven is going to be like earth?_____

_____

The Scriptures seem to say that heaven will be far beyond what we have ever seen. Heaven is going to be the most spectacular place ever! Skim through the book of Revelation and look for descriptions of heaven, God's throne, angels and other things you will see and hear in heaven. Describe the river of life.

_____

_____

Read Acts 7:42-50. Now go back and read some of the descriptions of the tabernacle (Exodus, chapters 25-40) and temple (1 Kings, chapters 1-10) that God directed his people to build. What are some of the materials God commanded to be used? How strict was God with how these were to be built?

_____

_____

Compare Acts 7:55 to Exodus 24:15-18.

2 Corinthians 5:1 says we will have a new building from God to replace our earthly tent. What do you think our earthly tent is?

_____

In My Own Words

_____

_____

_____

Talk to God

Heaven is going to be wonderful, Lord. I will have a new body and a new home. I will see You and Jesus. I will see all of the people who died and are with You already. I love You, God. Amen.

More of God's Word

2 Peter 3:13
Revelation, chapter 21

What I learned: _____

_____

The verse that best answered the question: _____

More questions: _____

_____

Words to Remember

But our citizenship is in heaven. And we eagerly await a Savior from there, the Lord Jesus Christ, who, by the power that enables him to bring everything under his control, will transform our lowly bodies so that they will be like his glorious body.
— Philippians 3:20-21

Is there really a hell?

Answers from the Word
Luke 16 19-31
Luke 12:4-5
Matthew 5:29-30
Matthew 18:9

Think About the Word

Look up and read all of the Scriptures above. Do they prove to you that there is really a hell? _____
_____

Look up John 3:16. Do you think that God wants to send anyone to hell? _____
_____

Read Matthew 16:18 at right. How strong is God's church?
_____

In My Own Words

_____
_____
_____

Talk to God

God, I realize that there really is a hell and that You don't want me to go there. You warn me in Your Word to follow Your ways. I will obey and serve and love You all my life. I will tell others so that they too will escape hell. Amen.

◎

More of God's Word

Matthew 5:29-30
Matthew 10:28
Ephesians 4:17-19

What I learned: _____

_____

The verse that best answered the question: _____

More questions: _____

_____

Words to Remember

And I tell you that you are Peter, and on this rock I will build my
church, and the gates of Hades will not overcome it.

— Matthew 16:18

⊙

Your Turn

Learn to search the Scriptures for answers to the questions you will have during your life! Follow the directions below to find your own answers in God's Word.

Write out your question here.

_____

_____

Answers from the Word

Use a Bible concordance. Look up several key words to help you find Scriptures to answer your question. For example, for the question "Who are God's enemies?" you would look up words like: enemies, ungodly and unbelievers.

Write out at least two or three Scriptures here. Try to find Scriptures that closely answer the question.

_____

_____

_____

_____

List some others you want to remember under "More of God's Word" at right.

Think About the Word

What does the Bible tell you? What did you learn?

_____

_____

_____

In My Own Words

Write out the answer to the question in your own words.

_____

_____

_____

_____

Talk to God

Write a prayer here.

_____

_____

_____

_____

More of God's Word

Use this space to list some extra Scriptures that you found above.

_____

_____

_____

_____

Words to Remember

After finding Scriptures to answer the question, write the best one here for you to memorize.

_____

_____

_____